The MAGIC BOWL
Parent's Guide

Published by Price World Publishing, LLC
1300 W. Belmont Ave, Suite 20G
Chicago, IL 60657

Book cover, design and layout by Raja Sekar R
Illustrations by Michal Arian
Editing by Jenn Sodini
Proofreading by Siobhán Gallagher
Printing by Malloy Incorporated

First Edition, May 2011
ISBN: 978-1-932549-64-5
Library of Congress Control Number: 2010932716

Printed in the United States of America
10 9 8 7 6 5 4 3 2 1

Dr. Baruch Kushnir's Toilet-Training System

A Parent's Guide

by
Dr. Baruch Kushnir, PhD
Clinical Psychologist

PRICE WORLD
PUBLISHING

Contents

What is special about this program?

In most cases, toilet training goes relatively smoothly. Sometimes, however, there can be mishaps along the way. The plan presented here allows for planning and preparation and puts the parents in control at every stage of the toilet-training process.

This program allows for a gradual progression that is in perfect harmony with the child. It teaches the necessary steps when a break in the process occurs. This program leads the child and parents down a clear path and minimizes the chance of setbacks, making it a positive experience by building the child's self-image, self-confidence, and overall mental development.

Introduction to Toilet Training

The toilet-training process varies between different cultures, families, siblings, and even twins. The common denominator is that almost all children eventually acquire habits of cleanliness and round-the-clock urinary and bowel control between the ages of one and three. It is important to remember that toilet training is a significant step in the development process of children. It is an opportunity to give children the basic feeling that they are loved and appreciated by their parents, even when failure or mishaps occur. **The process should be carried out in a positive atmosphere** that emphasizes success and avoids punishments, penalties, and expressions of anger and disappointment. A positive process contributes to strengthening the self-image and self-confidence of the child.

What is toilet training?

Toilet training is a process in which children move from evacuating whenever and wherever they feel necessary to maintaining control of these bodily functions and performing them at the appropriate time and place.

The toilet-training process is a step in the process of overall development. It symbolizes progress in gaining independence and control.

Like other developmental milestones, such as walking and speech, toilet training should be a positive and enjoyable experience for both child and parent.

It is important to remember that the personal comfort of the parents is secondary in this process. Toilet training cannot become a power struggle between the parents and the child. The child should not be allowed to control or dominate the

parents by rewarding or punishing them with compliance or defiance. Conversely, the parents should not punish a child out of frustration with the process, especially if the child is making his best effort.

Initiating the Toilet-Training Process

How is the process initiated?

The toilet-training process can begin in a wide variety of ways. Following are some examples:

Self-initiated

The child expresses his or her ability and desire to be like older family members and friends. He or she takes off the diaper and begins to use the toilet independently.

Parents' initiative

When parents notice signs of readiness, they stop the child from using a diaper, allowing the child to experience the unpleasantness of wetting and soiling himself. The parents then begin to guide and encourage the child to use the toilet.

Gradual ongoing initiatives

For a few weeks prior to stopping diaper usage, the parents expose their child to books and tapes on the subject, demonstrate by example, and encourage attempts to

use the toilet. As they observe the child's preparedness, they begin gradually to remove the diaper for longer periods of time and encourage the use of the toilet.

Intensified initiatives

It is generally recommended to use the above methods of initiating toilet training. The process is most successful when the pace is dictated by the child. Parents can try gently to move the process along by encouraging use of the bathroom, praising the child when he or she demonstrates an interest to stop using the diaper, and **avoiding any pressure.**

However, in rare cases, an intensive approach may be considered in order to expedite the process. This may be due to reasons such as: a requirement prior to entering school or kindergarten, the advancing age of the child, the child's distress by failure to complete the toilet-training process, or other circumstances that create the need to speed up the toilet-training process.

When an intensive program is called for, make sure that it is based on a coherent plan that is in harmony with the entire family in order to avoid creating conflicts with the child.

FAQs: Starting the Process

Do I have to wait until all signs of readiness appear?

Not necessarily. A comprehensive list of readiness tests is included in this manual. However, readiness and maturity in some areas is sufficient to start toilet training. This is a personal decision as well as a decision of judgment. It should be noted that, in some non-Western countries, the process is started prior to age one.

Am I ready for the toilet-training process?

You know if you are ready if you have recognized the need for patience and have the ability to practice it. This is not something that can be rushed. You must also be physically healthy. Do not initiate this process under physical or emotional duress.

If my child is ready, is there a preferred situation or season to start the toilet-training process?

It is best to begin the toilet-training process during warmer seasons, when children are

dressed in lighter clothing that is easier to remove. At the beginning of the process, it is best to set aside a period of three weeks in which the parent can give the child the time and attention necessary.

When should I not begin the process?

Do not begin the process during periods of transition, change, stress, and illness. Even small changes, such as a new babysitter, can impact the success of the child.

If I start the toilet-training process before my child is ready, will it hurt my child?

Yes. Any such process should be treated with the child's ability in mind. Avoid requests that cannot be met. A child's low self-image and self-confidence will have a negative effect on the process of toilet training.

Can postponing the toilet-training process be harmful?

Yes. Unnecessarily delaying the process can have physical, emotional, and social consequences. The child may not be able to participate in various activities with his peers and, in some cases, may not be accepted into schools or kindergartens. This can damage a child's self-confidence.

The Step by Step Training Plan

Important Information

Before implementing the plan, it is strongly advised that you read through the entire manual.

The plan presented here is based on the parents initiating the first step toward implementation of the toilet-training process.

The plan does not have to be carried out to the letter. There is room for improvisation, and changes can be applied as you see fit. Each child tends to progress at a different pace, so one must always consider the individual situation.

It is very important that parents go through the toilet-training process in complete harmony with the child, all the while providing positive encouragement and praise without any confrontation or pressure. When faced with opposition or refusal from the child, parents must stop and think of a pleasant way to circumvent the obstacle. If you cannot find a non-aggressive solution, you may have to halt the process or even go back a step or two.

Step One: Readiness

Are there signs that clearly display the child's readiness to be toilet trained and show that he or she is particularly motivated to stop using a diaper? It should be emphasized that testing for readiness continues throughout the process.

How do I know if my child is ready?

Your child is ready when he or she is physically and mentally ready. Here are some examples of readiness tests:

Physical readiness

Gross motor skills: the ability to perform physical movements like standing up, walking, lifting, and lowering hands.

Fine motor skills: the ability to perform delicate finger movements such as handling buttons or zippers, pulling pants up and down, lifting and lowering the toilet seat cover, and using toilet paper.

Physiological maturity: the brain and muscles are sufficiently developed. The child must be able to control his bladder

and sphincter and has the ability to stay dry and clean for at least two or three hours. In addition, the child can recognize and announce when his diaper is wet or soiled.

Health: child is physically free of illness.

Mental readiness

Personality: expresses the need for independence and has the motivation to get rid of the diaper and wear pants like a "big kid."

Communication: the ability to understand

what is being said, and to express desires in words.

Perceptual: understands simple cause and effect relationships, understands the order of operations, and is able to follow simple instructions such as "go to the bathroom."

Step Two: Preparing the Ground

Purchase a potty seat

Use the type of potty seat that fits on top of the toilet instead of a standalone potty. The potty seat is better because it closely resembles what the child will use in the future. Only use a standalone potty if the child expresses a clear preference for it. In these cases, aspire to gradually move the process from a potty to a toilet.

Purchase a toilet-training doll

This is a type of doll that can be filled with water to simulate urination. These dolls usually come with a bottle, underwear, a diaper, and a potty. A toilet-training doll is essential for the implementation of this plan. Get a good quality doll. Do not get a doll that empties the water automatically. Instead, select one in which a button has to be pressed to simulate urination.

Prepare some rewards

Gather a large stock of small prizes such as colored stickers, balloons, small toys, and other little things that can cheer up the child.

Stock up on supplies

During the first weeks of the process, you are going to want to have some extra things on hand: a spare set of clothes, toilet paper, wet-naps, plastic bags, and anything else that can help in case of an "accident." Being prepared will reduce inconvenience, embarrassment, and stress.

Protect bedding and furniture

Special protective sheets can save a lot of cleaning and washing work. Protective sheets that are super-absorbent can be

29

used to protect car seats, sofas, carpets, and other furniture.

Get the word out

Be proactive and inform the people that the child frequently comes in contact with (grandparents, kindergarten staff, siblings, babysitters) about the toilet-training process. Make sure their attitude about toilet training your child is consistent with your approach.

Step Three: Preparing the Child

Educate the child

Several weeks before starting the toilet-training process, begin to expose the child to books and tapes on the subject. Teach the child about his or her bodily functions and explain that these have to be done in the bathroom. Spend some time each day on the subject and gauge the child's reaction. Choose a long weekend or a few days during the week to dedicate to the subject.

Take the child underwear shopping

Have a "field trip" to the store to buy underwear. Allow the child to actively participate in the selection of colors and styles. Purchase a large number of underwear–twenty to thirty pairs–as you will need to change underwear often in the beginning. Time should not be wasted on washing and drying. A sufficient inventory will reduce the pressure on parents.

Step Four: Training

Begin the process by helping the child teach the doll to go in the toilet. In the first phase, the doll still wears a diaper. Suggest removing the diaper because the doll needs to learn to go in the toilet.

Together with the child, remove the doll's diaper and replace it with underwear. Fill the doll with water and begin role-playing with the doll. Playing the role of the doll, the parent should announce a need to go to the bathroom. Praise the doll for realizing the urge and ask it to go in the toilet. Take the child and doll into the bathroom. Once you've simulated going in the toilet, compliment the doll and award it a small prize, such as a colorful sticker.

Fill the doll with water again. Continue to play different games, and again repeat the part where the doll announces the need to go to the toilet.

Repeat the process several times for three or four hours. Give the child a central role in handling the doll. Allow the child to train it to flush, wash its hands, and award it prizes.

Every half hour or so, inspect the doll's underwear and compliment it for maintaining dryness. Focus the compliments around its ability to maintain dry underwear. Occasionally award it a small prize.

During this time, continue to offer the child liquids in order to fill his or her bladder, creating the need to go. In many cases, the child will express a desire to be like the doll and remove his or her diaper as well. Otherwise, about three hours into the process, gently invite the child to join

in and remove his or her own diaper, just like the doll.

Do not push or pressure the child and do not try excessive persuasion attempts. Parents must demonstrate that that the focus is on the child's wishes and not solely their own desires.

Your next move depends on the child's response.

If the child refuses to continue to participate with the doll, stop the simulation until the child demonstrates a desire to continue.

If the child participates willingly, remove the diaper and put on a pair of the new underwear.

Along with the doll, take the child to the bathroom every half hour and have the child sit on the toilet for about five minutes.

Praise the child every time he goes in the toilet.

Encourage him to let you know when he feels the urge.

Every half hour, check the underwear and compliment the child whenever he is dry. Praise and awards for a job well done are very important during this process.

Continue to check the underwear and accompany the child and the doll to the bathroom.

When you notice significant progress in the child's reaction, begin to reduce interference by waiting longer in between interventions. As the process continues, gradually lengthen the period of time

between checks from a half hour to one and a half hours.

You will notice a gradual increase in independence and development as the child takes part in all initiatives related to using the toilet, finally achieving complete toilet training.

It is okay to have a setback once in a while. Expect ups and downs. Setbacks happen even after several days or weeks of control. In such cases, do not express frustration or anger, and avoid confrontation with the child. Try to be understanding and encouraging. Stick to the plan.

Also, using small prizes such as charts, stickers, and candy can maintain a child's interest in the process.

There is always room for cheers, encouragement, praise, and compliments.

Remember that the big prize in the process of withdrawal is to be clean, dry, and diaper-free.

How and when to teach how to wipe?

Wiping is an integral part of the toilet-training process. Teaching wiping is difficult for many parents because the errors associated with it are very unpleasant.

Start with a demonstration and explanation, preferably with the doll.

Teach the child to use paper until the paper is clean.

41

Allow small steps with supervision. Continue to supervise wiping, gradually reducing your interventions until the child is successful.

Be prepared to deal with failures.

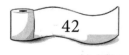

FAQs: Typical problems in the process of toilet training

What do I do when my child expresses fear of the toilet's water?

This is a common problem with many children. First, try throwing a few pieces of toilet paper down the toilet and let the child himself flush and watch the process.

Place a few sheets of toilet paper on top of the water in the bowl. This will reduce the sense of depth, the sound of rushing water, and splashes.

Explain again the process of how food and water turn into feces and urine. This will foster a better understanding of bodily functions and soothe any fears of separation anxiety.

What if my child becomes constipated during the toilet training process?

You should check the child's food consumption. Children whose diets consist primarily of meat, rice, potatoes, and sweets tend to develop severe constipation.

Parents should add vegetables, fruit, fiber, and water to the child's diet.

Contact your pediatrician if the problem persists.

What should I do when my child experiences mishaps immediately after leaving the toilet?

This is a common phenomenon at the beginning of the toilet-training process. It usually disappears after a few days. If

it continues on a regular basis, it means that the child is not ready to be toilet trained. Parents should stop the process, reintroduce the diaper, and wait several weeks before trying again.

What if my child wants someone with him when he sits on the toilet?

This too is a common phenomenon at the beginning of the toilet-training process. Do not allow your child to rely on one particular person. Provide your child

with activities like coloring books or toys. The supervising adult should gradually withdraw himself or herself (using excuses if necessary) until the child is independent in the bathroom.

When should I turn to professional help?

Consult a professional if your child is still untrained at three or four years old, after you have tried all the usual methods.

Also turn to a professional if there is evidence of any unusual behavior that may cause physical or mental damage.

How should I respond to mishaps?

Toilet training is a continuous process with ups and downs; there will be mishaps. Parents must recognize their own feelings of anger and disappointment and avoid expressing them to the child.

Respond with encouragement and solace, thereby calming the child.

When should I stop the toilet-training process and take a break for a while?

Halt the process if the conditions change, if the parent or child falls ill, or if you encounter a particularly complex obstacle like constipation.

Stopping the process and returning to use of diapers, when reality demands it, does not cause any damage. You can always start over and complete the withdrawal process successfully.

Dry Nights

Becoming dry at night is a natural process that occurs by itself, usually without parental intervention. Bowel movements at night stop naturally. This usually happens in the early stages of the toilet-training process.

Bladder control at night comes to most children spontaneously.

When do I remove the diaper at night?

Remove the diaper when you notice that the child repeatedly wakes up in the morning with a dry diaper.

Should I automatically remove the nighttime diaper while toilet training?

Many parents tend to remove the nighttime diaper along with the daytime diapers. In some cases, the mere removal of the diaper hastens the toilet-training process and the number of dry nights.

However, in those cases where the child goes three weeks without a dry night, parents should use a diaper or seek professional help for a bed-wetting solution. There is no point in continuing to endure the effects of bed-wetting. One can always try to remove the diaper again later on.

Of course, parents must explain to the child the reasons for this step. This must not be perceived as a punishment or an act of humiliation.

Night training should resume in a few months.

How do I protect the bedding during the process?

Use special protective sheets.

Should I limit my child's drinking before bedtime?

No. The child should be allowed to drink as he pleases.

Should I make my child use the toilet before bed?

No. You may mention or suggest it, but do not demand it.

Should I wake my child to use the bathroom during the night?

You can try waking the child for three weeks and then stop to monitor their progress. If wetting continues, then there is no point in waking the child. Simply return to using a diaper and try again after a few months.

In those cases where removal of the diaper is not effective, parents should also consider seeking professional help for a

bed-wetting solution. Modern approaches and technology enable successful treatment from ages as early as three.

The longer a child continues to wet his bed beyond the age of two and a half years old, the smaller his chances are of being able to stop without professional intervention. Twenty percent of all five-year-olds still wet their beds at night. The number decreases to two percent by age eighteen.

Chronic Bed-Wetting

Causes of bed-wetting

Research literature suggests that the main cause of bed-wetting is a congenital physiological dysfunction of the reflex system responsible for automatic control of the bladder.

There are a number of clear facts regarding bed-wetting:

1) There is a known element of heredity. In over seventy percent of bed-wetting cases, a parent, uncle, or aunt was a bed wetter.

2) Bed-wetting is more common among boys than girls.

3) In seventy percent of cases, bed-wetting is "primary," meaning the child never reaches a state of complete continence. In thirty percent of cases, bed-wetting is "secondary," meaning the child reaches complete continence at a certain age and then begins wetting again. In many cases, there is a recurrence of nocturnal enuresis (nighttime bed-wetting) following an identifiable event that causes emotional stress. This can be a change of residence, the birth of

a younger sibling, or a new school. In other cases, it is hard to pin-point any specific factor that brings about renewed nocturnal enuresis. Both types of bed-wetting respond well to appropriate treatment.

4) Incidence of the problem is higher in younger children and decreases gradually in older children. At two and a half years old, fifty percent of all children are still wetting themselves. By ages three and four, this number falls to twenty-five percent of all children. Twenty percent are still wetting themselves at the age of five.

5) Some twenty-five percent of all nighttime bed wetters also suffer from daytime wetting.

6) The child bed-wetting population does not present any special behavioral problems. This information is based on various research findings and on the vast amount of literature collected by this author. Nocturnal enuresis should not be seen as an expression of an emotional problem. Nonetheless, there is a connection between a person's emotional condition and nocturnal enuresis.

Common Misconceptions about Bed-Wetting

Bed-wetting is not caused by excessive consumption of fluids at bedtime

When the bladder control system functions well, there will never be an incident of uncontrollable discharge of urine during sleep. This is irrespective of the amount of fluids taken before bedtime. The child will either sleep through the night or be woken up by the pressure of the bladder to go to the bathroom.

Withholding or avoiding liquid intake before bedtime cannot offer a solution to the problem. Moreover, it can be harmful.

A child's body needs to stay hydrated. Also, by withholding liquids from the child, you are preventing the child's bladder from receiving the exercise it needs in order to achieve control. Furthermore, withholding liquids causes tension and dispute. A parent might misinterpret a child's insistence on a bedtime drink as a sign that the child is unwilling to cooperate in solving the bedwetting problem.

Bed-wetting is not the result of exhaustion or lack of sleep.

It is a mistake to try to treat the problem by changing a child's sleeping habits. The child should not be forced to take a nap in the afternoon, nor should he be forced to go to bed earlier in the evening.

Bed-wetting is not caused by avoiding the toilet before going to bed.

Many parents of bed-wetting children insist they pay a visit to the toilet at

bedtime, which is often a source of anger and stress.

Children sometimes refuse simply because they do not feel the need to go at that particular moment. Parents of these children are advised to treat this subject just as they do during the day–the child visits the toilet alone, and in accordance with his or her own decision. In other words, using the toilet before going to sleep does not, in itself, constitute a way of treating the problem.

Bed-wetting is not caused by deep sleep.

There are many children (and adults), who sleep heavily and do not wet their beds at night. However, excessively deep sleep, although not the cause of bed-wetting, can hinder treatment of the problem. When treated properly, sound sleep will no longer present an obstacle to effective training.

Bed-wetting is not caused by climate factors alone.

There have been cases reported of increased wetting during periods of

fluctuating weather. However, it is clear that the weather is not the reason behind the problem; it only serves as a catalyst.

If it seems that bladder control is disturbed in response to weather changes, and this continues for a prolonged length of time, this may be the result of a urinary tract infection and a doctor should be consulted.

Bed-wetting is not usually the result of an illness or anatomical defect in the nervous system or the urinary tract.

Nonetheless, it recommended that the family's pediatrician be consulted for an accurate diagnosis.

Dealing with Bed-Wetting

Reactions to the problem, as well as the treatment plan, will differ from family to family and child to child. It can be influenced by different factors such as the child's age, parental expectations of the child, the child's attitude towards the problem, a parent's experience with older siblings, and the personal experiences of the parents. Children who are especially

troubled by the problem, and show a desire and willingness to overcome it, will often experience less criticism and blame on the part of their parents.

These issues can play out in several ways. For example, parents who themselves stopped wetting their beds at a later age might be more patient and understanding. Conversely, these parents could have the mistaken belief that nothing can be done and that their child is destined to wet the bed until at least the same age that they did. Notwithstanding these differences, it is possible to pin-point experiences

and concepts that are common to many families.

When a child continues to wet the bed at night, at an age when diurnal (daytime) bladder control has been achieved, most parents hope that the problem will solve itself, and soon. In many cases it does. When their hopes are not realized, when years go by and the child still wets the bed at night, parents start hoping that their child will solve the problem on his own. They remind the child to pay a visit to the toilet before going to bed. They plead to the child to demonstrate control at night.

They explain to the child that he or she is a "big boy" or "big girl" and that it's not nice to wet the bed. They promise awards for a dry night, and even try to help by leading the child to the toilet in the middle of the night. When these methods fail, their feelings of anger and frustration increase and are expressed in negative comments. These frustrations can gradually turn into real expressions of anger, threats, ridicule, punishment, and even physical violence. When these reactions do not bring about any improvement in the situation, parents try to ignore it, hoping in this way to achieve salvation. When nothing seems to

Never limit drinking before bedtime.

**Never force a child to visit the bathroom
before bedtime.**

help, parents often simply give up. At some stage or another during the process, parents turn to their pediatrician. Pediatricians' attitudes to the problem of nocturnal enuresis are not universal. Usually, the doctor will carry out basic tests on the child to rule out the possibility of urinary tract infections, an anatomic malfunction in the urinary mechanism, or a malfunction in the nervous system connected to it. More often than not, these tests prove that the problem is not a medical one. It is at this stage that parents become exposed to a wide variety of confusing and sometimes conflicting potential solutions. This advice

is usually limited at best, and the solutions are often temporary. In most cases, the family is stuck with the problem.

As for the child himself, nocturnal enuresis is a source of emotional and physical pain and suffering. From an emotional point of view, the child experiences a constant sense of failure and shame for being unable to function in the same way as his peers. He or she feels like a disappointment to parents and siblings and is constantly aware of their anger and blame. The child lives in constant fear of having the "secret" revealed. Many times the child is obliged

to give up field trips and sleepovers. He or she is socially restricted and feels lonely, frustrated, and dejected. If unchecked, this condition can cause irreversible damage to the child's self-confidence, self-image, and the normal development of personality. In terms of physical distress, the bed-wetting child has to experience the discomfort of wet bedding, the nuisance of having to change sheets every day, the smell of urine first thing in the morning, and the frequent rashes and skin irritations that are the result of lying in urine-soaked sheets.

The child's family suffers as well. There is the daily routine of doing laundry, the annoyance of wet sheets and pajamas, and the unpleasant smell of urine in the bedroom and the rest of the home. The fear of "accidents" becomes an important element in planning family outings and visits to foreign places. Often it presents a significant hindrance to the family's day-to-day life.

The Importance of Treating Bed-Wetting at an Early Age

Bed-wetting is a serious infliction both to children and to their families.

When it continues for a long time, it is damaging both to the child and to his relationships with parents and siblings.

When a child between the age of three and four is still regularly wetting the bed, it is time for parents to seek professional help.

Treatment using a bed-wetting alarm

There is a consensus among most enuresis experts that the bedwetting alarm is the simplest and most effective method for overcoming the problem, provided that it is applied under professional guidance and follow-up.

The modern enuresis alarm is a small, two-part instrument that consists of a tiny sensor, which is attached to the user's underpants, and a small wireless alarm unit placed in the child's room.

The alarm unit is activated the moment wetting begins, as soon as the first drop of urine touches the sensor. This causes the

child to awaken and get up and go to the toilet.

Treatment using a bed-wetting alarm is based on the principle of Classical Conditioning. When the automatic bladder control system is in order, the full bladder arouses a response of muscle contraction, which prevents the escape of urine. Alternately, an extremely full bladder results in its owner awakening from sleep. When the system is not in order, the full bladder does not produce any response. The result is bed-wetting. When a bed-wetting child is awakened at the very

moment that the bladder is overflowing, he or she immediately reacts by exercising self-control.

The conditioning action of the alarm method is as follows:

Full bladder + an awakening alarm = awakening + control

This action, repeated night after night, brings us to next stage:

Full bladder = full control

When the child is being treated with the alarm method, he is awakened at the exact moment that wetting begins and is obliged to stop, get out of bed, and go to the toilet. When this action is repeated consistently, night after night, the child's bladder control system is reinforced and begins to gradually operate on its own. The child becomes gradually dry until he reaches a stage of complete dryness at night, either because he or she is able to sleep through the night, or because the full bladder causes the child to arise. In both cases, there is no longer any uncontrolled wetting of the bed. A full, detailed description and an animation film demonstrating this treatment intervention can be viewed at **www.dr-kushnir.com**.

An Adult Bed Wetter's Story

Nocturnal enuresis is a serious infliction to both children and their families. When it continues for a long time, it is damaging both to the child and to his relationship with his parents and siblings. The following is an excerpt from a letter I received from a woman named Angela who was twenty-five years old when she came to me for therapy:

"My name is Angela. I am single and live with my parents. From early childhood I have suffered from nocturnal enuresis. My bed-wetting has caused me to be hypersensitive, afraid of forming relationships with men, afraid to sleep away from home, and many other emotional pressures (although various therapists have claimed that nocturnal enuresis is a result of my emotional problems). My parents did nothing to solve my problem when I was a child, both due to lack of awareness and because my older sister stopped wetting her bed shortly before she began her military service, and they believed that my problem would solve itself in the same way. But the situation deteriorated as my own enlistment drew near. I wanted nothing more than to be stationed far away from home—to get the real feel of being in the

Army–but I was obliged to do my service in the vicinity of my hometown. In fact, the Army would not have enlisted me at all had I revealed my bed-wetting problem. After the service, I learned that there are (a few) places which deal with this problem. Of course I went and I tried, but nothing helped. On the contrary, I suffered great anguish at the hands of the doctor, who never missed the chance to blame me for neglecting my problem and accused me of not wanting to put an end to it. This stressed me even more. I will never forget this terrible period in my life. I was afraid of being insulted again and did not want

to go for any more treatments. My sister was very supportive, and she convinced me that I had nothing to lose. So I gathered all my willpower and I made an appointment with Dr. Kushnir. Now, after four months of treatment, I am very proud to say that I am finally completely dry. I must admit that my whole life has changed. I have my self-confidence back and I know now that one should never give up hope."

Daytime Incontinence

Daytime enuresis is a condition in which there is an uncontrolled release of urine while awake. Twenty-five percent of children who suffer from bed-wetting also have the problem of urine escaping during daytime waking hours. It usually presents itself as a gradual dripping of urine. This condition does not usually involve full-scale urination into their clothes. The child who wets himself during the day can be identified by wet patches on his lower garments.

Oftentimes a child suffering this condition displays a tendency to procrastinate going to the toilet. When he is asked to go to the toilet, he usually makes an excuse to not go. This kind of behavior is very annoying because it gives the impression that the child is able to control the situation, but chooses to wet the clothes out of carelessness or laziness. In fact, it is not as simple as it seems. Everyone knows how difficult it is to draw a child's attention away from the television, a game, or something else the child may be engrossed in. Yet most of these children do not wet their clothes. Furthermore, it is important to remember

that daytime enuresis is almost always accompanied by nocturnal enuresis; it is very rare for it to be a symptom on its own. Daytime enuresis is usually connected to the same dysfunction of the reflex system that causes nocturnal enuresis.

Children and adults who are not enuretic during the day receive a sharp and clear message with regard to an increased pressure on the bladder, and they respond accordingly by activating voluntary muscles or by paying a visit to the toilet. In any case, these people do not experience an escape of urine into their clothes. It would

seem that the message received by daytime enuretics, on the other hand, is duller and that their response is therefore different, and this allows for an escape of urine into their clothes. This problem could also be the result of a problem or an infection in the urinary tract. A visit should be made to the pediatrician, who will make the correct diagnosis and offer suitable treatment. It should be pointed out that diurnal enuresis usually disappears simultaneously with treatment for bed-wetting. In rare cases only is it necessary for treatment to focus solely on daytime wetting. An effective intervention is presented here.

Treatment of daytime wetting

In cases of daytime wetting, it is recommended that the parents first consult a physician, who will make a diagnosis and eliminate the possibility of physical dysfunction, infection, or disease. Once these factors have been eliminated, a treatment can be applied.

In order to reduce the occurrence of diurnal wetting, it is necessary for parents to take their child to the toilet every hour or hour and a half during the day. The word "take" is stressed here, in the sense that the child has to be physically taken to the toilet and told that he or she must try to urinate. It must be clear that it is not a suggestion. The child must not be asked if he or she wants to go, nor should the child be reminded to go. All these cause the child to refuse, prevaricate, or argue and, in the end, wet his clothes again, which results in frustration and anger on the part of his parents. Thus the child must be taken firmly by the hand and led to the toilet, no questions asked. When the parents are firm and convinced of their actions, and do not capitulate to the child, the child will realize after a day or two that

the safest and fastest way to get back to his or her own affairs is to cooperate with the parents and go to the toilet when told to do so. This kind of routine succeeds in bringing about a sharpening of the senses in the urinary control system and prompts the child to take his own initiative and go to the toilet, thereby achieving a solution to the problem of daytime wetting.

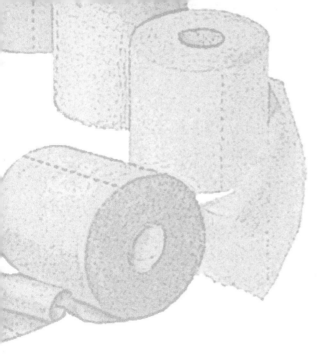

Questions to Dr. Kushnir

Question One

"I have a two-and-a-half-year-old daughter who has been toilet training for five weeks. In the early stages she had many mishaps, both pooping and peeing in her pants. Halfway through the process, the mishaps increased. Recently, she stopped asking to go. She just goes in her pants–anywhere, anytime–and will not sit on a potty or toilet. It's as if she is afraid. All of a sudden, she is not really ready to sit on the toilet or potty. I don't make it an issue or force her. On the contrary, I praise her all the time and let her move slowly at her own pace. Her kindergarten teacher says she pees in her pants on purpose if she does not get what she wants–that it is her way of being in control. My daughter is very smart and understands well that peeing and pooping is to be done in the toilet. She would actually say that if you ask her. Sometimes she sits on the toilet, all on her own, without any prompting from me. When she has mishaps that end up on the floor, she says, "I peed on the floor." If I ask, "Where should you have done that?" she says, "In the potty." I'm very patient with

her and I don't get angry. But lately, as I don't see any progress, I feel very frustrated and discouraged. I don't understand what made her change like that. Why does she not want to sit on the toilet anymore? What am I doing wrong, and what should I do to continue the process efficiently and quickly to resolve this issue?"

Answer One

It is very important that you are aware of your frustration and always in control of your emotions. The toilet-training process must not become a source of anger and

conflict with your child. Toilet training is often characterized by ups and downs, as well as changes in the child's behavior. It is very important that parents maintain a harmonious atmosphere by being even-tempered and in sync with the child's pace, thereby preventing it from becoming the cause of anger and confrontation. Always keep in mind that potty training is the child's own process, and that he has no obligation to proceed according to the parent's timetable.

As I see it, it seems that the child was not really ready to separate from the diaper in

the first place, and that the decision to start the toilet training was initiated by you, albeit too early. Under these circumstances, I advise you to take a few steps back and return to using a diaper, thereby removing the pressure on the child and the family.

Wait until you see clear signs of readiness from the child. Coordinate your efforts with others, such as the daycare teacher. Follow a clear plan.

Question Two

"My daughter is three years and two months old, and her story is somewhat out of the

ordinary. During the summer of 2008, we began the process of toilet training. It was going pretty well. We had whole days without a diaper, and she pooped and peed in the potty or toilet. Following an illness, there was a significant regression in the process. I was pregnant and didn't have the energy to clean the puddles off of the floor, so I decided to put her back in diapers. In the past six months, she has gone through a lot—she became an older sister, we returned home after years abroad to a new residence, and her grandmother, with whom she was very attached to, died. It was way too much for a little girl. I feel now that we

have fallen into a new routine, it is time to restart toilet training. Although I am emotionally available and have the time to devote to her, she will not have any part of it. She says she is still too little and does not want to say goodbye to her diapers–not ever. I'm not pressuring her, but I wonder how I should proceed, and how to convince her to restart the process. Do I force her or follow her lead? She is not going to daycare yet. She is at home with me."

Answer Two

There are no clear rules regarding the perfect time for toilet training. According to your description, the child has recently gone through a lot and her attitude towards toilet training is completely understandable. Since there is no particular reason that would require you to act urgently, I advise you continue to wait patiently for the child to show signs of readiness. Just let nature take its course and remove any pressure off of you and the child. When the need arises for you to initiate toilet training, be sure to follow a clear and a well-planned program.

Question Three

"My daughter is two and ten months old. For about a month, she's been pooping in the toilet every morning on her own initiative. It looks like she's ready to be toilet trained, at least according to her promises. However, in spite of it all, she continues to go in her diaper. It should be noted that sometimes, to our surprise, she asks to go in the toilet. This happens even in school. I don't know how to speed up the process. I feel I still cannot get rid of the diaper, since she still wets in it. What should I do?"

Answer Three

Your daughter is going through a natural process. She has taken a few steps forward and a few back. This is absolutely normal; many children experience the same. I strongly recommend letting her be so she may proceed on her own schedule, in her own way. There is no need to speed up the process and force her to make promises that she may not be able to keep. Praise her when appropriate, in a reasonable manner and without exaggeration.

Question Four

"My daughter is three and one-half years old, and has been toilet trained (during the day) for a little less than a year now. However, nighttime is a different story. Up until nearly six months ago, she went to bed with a diaper on but would take it off in the middle of the night. Then we decided to remove the diaper at night. Most nights were dry, but for several months now she has wet her bed almost every night. She wakes up, I clean her, and she goes back to sleep. It's important to note that her little sister was born six months ago. She refuses

to pee before bed time. Aside from the fact that I am exhausted from doing laundry so many times, I do not know what this is doing to her self-image. I was told to offer her a diaper at night again, but I am afraid she'd be insulted."

Answer Four

Most bed-wetting children recover naturally without any intervention from the parents. Parents can speed up this natural process by some intervention. In this case, I would suggest discontinuing

use of a diaper. Here are some guidelines if you are going to try this method.

- Stop using a diaper for the next three weeks.

- Allow the child to go to bed without a diaper.

- Allow the child to drink freely during the evening and before bedtime.

- Encourage the child to go to the bathroom before bedtime, but without undue pressure.

- Avoid waking the child to go to the bathroom during the night.

- Track bed-wetting events.

If the number of dry nights gradually goes up, then the child is going through the natural process and will be completely dry over time.

If the child continues to wet with no change in three weeks, most likely the natural process is not taking place. In this case, you have two options. You can either go back to using a diaper and try again in a few months, or you can use a bed-

wetting alarm under the supervision of a professional.

Treatment with a bed-wetting alarm is considered the most effective solution for the problem, according to the *Nelson Textbook of Pediatrics*, commonly believed to be the world's leading authority in pediatric medicine. However, it is essential to use this device with professional counseling and support. The success rate of the alarm alone is only fifteen percent, compared with a ninety percent success rate when it is used in conjunction with professional instruction and guidance.

Question Five

"My son is three years old, and has been peeing in the toilet since the age of two. The problem is pooping. He is not willing to go in the toilet or potty. He only goes in his pants and in the corner of the room. I have managed to convince him to sit on the toilet with rewards (candy). However, he eats the candy, and still doesn't go. He actually poops in his pants as soon as I take him off the toilet. There was a time in which he would go in the toilet at school, but not at home.

Now he no longer goes in the toilet at school either. I want to specify that during the toilet training period, there were a few significant changes: change of residence, a new school, and the birth of his new brother. This has been a very frustrating situation and it is beginning to create arguments between me and my husband."

Answer Five

You are describing a complex problem. You, the parents, must agree to form a united front to deal with the problem. You must avoid being drawn into conflicts

and arguments between the two of you—it makes solving the problem that much more complicated. One possible approach that might help solve the problem is this: after the child goes in his pants, sit him on the toilet with his clothes on and drop the poop directly from his clothes into the toilet. Let him flush the toilet and praise him every time it happens. It is very possible that he will get used to this routine and move a step forward to go completely in the toilet. However, as stated before, this is a complex problem. If this approach doesn't work, I suggest you seek more in-depth professional help.

Question Six

"My son is three and nine months old. He has been peeing in the toilet for a year now, and during that year that we have tried to train him to also poop in the toilet. Our efforts have produced varied results. He continued to wear a diaper for a long time. Six months ago, he changed to wearing regular underwear, yet he has continued to poop in his pants. Sometimes, because we pressure him, he goes in the toilet, but he almost never takes the initiative. Tomorrow he begins a new preschool that requires children to be completely toilet trained,

and I don't know what to do. We tried all the methods known to mankind and even went to consult a child psychologist. My child is very smart and well-developed cognitively and emotionally for his age. I'm exhausted and I am not even thinking of beginning night training, as he goes to bed wearing a diaper and wakes up with a soaked one every morning. He has a little brother, who is two years old, and my husband spends a lot of time away on business. Is there another method that I haven't tried yet? Should I just relax and let the process come naturally? For how long? Until age five?"

Answer Six

Generally speaking, your approach must be one that will reduce the stress that you and your child are experiencing. For bed-wetting, you can immediately implement the use of a bed-wetting alarm. This would solve the problem of wetting at night and contribute to the child's feelings of success and pride for all issues related to sphincter control.

Regarding the soiling issue–you have to sit the child on the toilet every time he poops in his pants and empty the poop into the

toilet. Let the child flush the toilet and praise him on this accomplishment. At the same time, try to direct him to go in the toilet when he feels the urge. Remember to praise him when he goes in the toilet. In your case, quality time with you can be very effective. Plan to dedicate time for him alone, as it is possible that this problem stems from a feeling that attention is being directed away from him and given to his little brother. It is important to avoid reactions of anger and frustration.

Question Seven

"I have a daughter that is two years and nine months. We started potty training five months ago, when I was seven months pregnant. I gave birth a month-and-a-half ago. Regardless, she continues to pee and poop in her pants, some days more frequently than others. I don't think that these are mishaps; I think she is doing it deliberately. What should I do?"

Answer Seven

It seems that the toilet-training process you have tried for so long is not effective. You should contact your doctor. Analyze the situation carefully, identify the obstacles, and then build a cohesive plan that will lead to desired results. Avoid blaming the child for failure or accusing her of doing it on purpose. These interpretations do not help the toilet-training process, and they may harm your relationship with the child, as well as her self-image and self-confidence.

Question Eight

"My daughter is one year and eight months old. I felt she was ready to be toilet trained, so I started the process last week. Within three days she started to pee in a potty. She even went in the toilet once. On a couple of occasions, we went out and I made her wear a diaper, since at that moment she would not go in the potty or toilet. The problem is that she does not tell me when she has to go. It seems to me that I have ruined the process and made her resistant. Should I discontinue and give up now? Wait until

she asks for it? I feel guilty for ruining the process. What should I do?"

Answer Eight

Perhaps indeed it was a mistake to allow the child to use a diaper that day. As parents we try to do the best for our children, but we all make mistakes. We have to accept that fact with love and understanding. According to the child's behavior, it seems that she was not quite ready to stop using the diaper. Therefore, it only makes sense to back up and use a diaper again. There

will be another opportunity in the future when you will see clear signs of readiness.

Question Nine

"My daughter is one year and nine months old, highly developed cognitively, understands everything, and speaks fluently. Physically, she has developed very slowly; she is not able to take off her pants without losing her balance and falling. She entered daycare at the beginning of the year. Would you recommend waiting to potty train her until after the beginning of

the school year, when she has had time to get acclimated?"

Answer Nine

Decidedly, yes–I would suggest waiting. Always wait until you see clear indications that the child is ready to be toilet trained.

Question Ten

"My son is two-and-a-half. We started the process of toilet training three months ago, which is when he showed signs of readiness. I was eight months pregnant, and three

days into the toilet-training process, the daycare teacher recommended we stop training him because, in her opinion, he would surely regress after I gave birth. So we stopped and then started again about a month after I delivered. Now he refuses to sit on the potty or the toilet, and will not let us know when he needs to go. He will sit on the toilet but only after he's already gone in his pants. What do I do? It has been two weeks of no progress, and waiting longer seems unrealistic, as he will be three years old soon. I think that we made a mistake by stopping the first time."

Answer Ten

Under the current situation, I recommend that you use a diaper. The child is still not quite ready to be toilet trained. Wait until you see clear signs of the child's desire to toilet train and his readiness to be without a diaper. When you initiate toilet training in the future, follow a planned program with clear guidelines.

Question Eleven "My daughter is three-and-a-half and is not yet potty trained. She's not motivated to be toilet trained, and seems to like going in the diaper. Even

124

when the diaper is full, it doesn't seem to bother her. In addition, she has constipation issues. We were told this is a result of her jealousy towards her newborn brother. I tried removing her diaper, but had to put it back on, as it seemed she had no control. She didn't mind wearing the diaper again. What do I do? Should I keep trying or wait until she shows initiative on her part?"

Answer Eleven

Regarding the constipation issue, please contact your pediatrician. It is possible that

the child may need a change in her diet or a dietary supplement.

Regarding toilet training, it seems that the girl has not yet shown signs of readiness. Wait until you see some clear signs. Meanwhile, use a diaper. It is very possible that the issue of jealousy is creating a significant obstacle to potty training and causing developmental and behavioral issues. Particular attention should be given to her because time has been taken away from her and given to the newborn. It is recommended that she spends as much quality time as possible with you and her

father. You may also want to consider an in-depth professional consultation.

Question Twelve

"My daughter is two years and seven months old. She's been toilet trained for a week, both day and night. She seems to be holding for too long while watching TV or playing a game. She has a few mishaps per day, and at times will start going in her pants and then will finish in the toilet. In my opinion, she is holding back for hours. How do I convince her to let me know when she feels the urge?"

Answer Twelve

Usually toilet training is a gradual and continuous process, with many ups and downs. The symptoms you describe are common and typical at the beginning of the process. Avoid exerting pressure on her and creating confrontations. The situation can be improved by gently encouraging the child to drink larger amounts of liquids and praising her occasionally (not every time) when she takes the initiative to go to the bathroom. You can also check her pants once in a while and praise her for being clean and dry. Be patient, as there

haven't been many occurrences since the beginning of the process. These symptoms do not represent a serious problem.

Question Thirteen

"My son is two years and three weeks old. He asks to remove the diaper and sit on the toilet when he feels the urge to poop. He sits down and then gets up several times, until finally (in most cases) he poops on the floor while standing up. We try to encourage him, but he seems to be afraid of sitting down on the toilet. Regarding peeing, he never lets us know,

neither before nor after. Is he ready to be toilet trained? Is there a sequence of events necessary for correct toilet training? Pee first, poop second? Please help."

Answer Thirteen

It seems that the child finds interest in trying to use the toilet on his own and testing his own ability. Praise him for every attempt. You should try to expose him to books and videos on the subject and allow him to progress at his own pace, without having to intervene directly or pressure him. The sequence of events in his progress

is not very important, and makes little difference. It seems that in his case, the sequence of the toilet-training process is changing so much. Let him proceed in his own style.

Question Fourteen

"My daughter is one year and seven months old, and I have begun the process of toilet training. Is this a good age to start potty training? She still does not understand why she's sitting on the toilet. Is this normal in the early stages of potty training? Thanks."

Answer Fourteen

The question we need to be asking in this case is what exactly made you decide to start toilet training? Did the child specifically request it? Have you noticed clear signs that she was willing to be toilet trained, or was it your decision regardless of her developmental stage? Another question to consider is how to continue the toilet-training process that you initiated. Did you follow a clear plan as you should? Or did you simply remove the diaper and expect her to start using the toilet on her own?

It is very important to consider these questions closely, as you may have started the process too soon and may need to go back to using a diaper and restart the process several months from now.

Question Fifteen

"My son is almost three, and a very verbal, intelligent child, but he seems to be lost when it comes to toilet training. We tried to begin toilet training him over the holiday. We removed his diaper and took him to the bathroom, even when he said he didn't have to go. He asked a few times to

go on his own, but didn't have much come out. Needless to say, every time he goes we praise him and reward him. Since the holiday, we haven't seen real progress. We lost sight of our objective and returned to using a diaper while he is at daycare in the morning. Sometimes we remove it in the afternoon when he gets home. Last week he managed to do a little poop in the potty so we tried again with the teacher to begin potty training, but without success. He simply does not ask to go to the bathroom, he poops and pees in his pants, and now—in what seems to be a bigger problem—he refuses to change his dirty diaper. What do

we do? In theory he is aware of everything going on, as he talks about it. In a few months he is supposed to move up to pre-school, where he must be toilet trained to enter. I await your advice, or maybe a miracle."

Answer Fifteen

It's sad to think that the upcoming move to a school that requires toilet-trained children is a cause for tension and an artificial hastening of the natural developmental process. Toilet training should be accomplished calmly, based on

the child's readiness and ability. Try not to let this deadline influence your state of mind; act as if it doesn't exist. If there will be a problem and the child will not be toilet trained on time, find another school or system where he'll be accepted as is. The behavior you describe tells me that the child may not quite be ready to be toilet trained. I recommend that you go back to using the diaper and suggest that you do not pressure yourself or the child. If you feel that you need to expedite the process, do so based on a clear plan. A cohesive, cleverly-prepared plan based on professional advice, along

with cooperation from the teacher, could be just what you need.

Question Sixteen

"I have a three-year-old boy who pees in the toilet only when someone is standing next to him. I cannot reason with him at all regarding pooping; he will only go in a diaper. He refuses to go in the toilet. Sometimes he pees on the floor on purpose."

Answer Sixteen

A simulation of the process is in order. The child has to feel as close as possible to

the experience of going in the toilet. First, when he poops in the diaper, sit him on the toilet with the diaper and empty it into the toilet and then have him flush it down. Then prepare a new diaper with a cut along the bottom of it. This will allow you to tear the diaper in half when the child is seated on the toilet, letting the contents of the diaper drop into the toilet after he poops. This will make the experience similar to the real-life situation. In addition, prepare dough by adding cocoa (for brown color effect) to flour and water and put the dough into a plastic bag. Make a small hole in the bag and ask the child to press the dough

through the hole into the toilet. Have him flush the toilet. These two actions will simulate the real experience and will help him move forward in the process. Make sure the process is done in a fun way, and praise him after each positive action. This whole process should be accompanied by much laughter and joy.

Question Seventeen

"My daughter is two and ten months. She is a healthy, smart child and very lively. At the age of two and three months, three months after entering daycare, the teacher told me that she took off her diaper, walked around naked, and went to the bathroom independently. I was glad but surprised because we were only at the early stages of toilet training, and she had not yet shown willingness to quit using a diaper. I went along with it and bought her underwear and encouraged her, and she continued to be completely diaper-less at school. However, at home there were quite a lot of "accidents" and a distinct lack of desire to quit the diaper. I tried all winter to keep her without a diaper at home and encouraged her to go in the bathroom. I tried to talk

to her about it, showed her videos, and told her stories. I even tried ignoring it all together, but nothing changed–she still continues the same behavior. The teacher was very surprised to hear about her lack of progress at home. I have explained to her that I understand that she does not want to behave at home as she does at school, and therefore I have put her in diapers again. I told her that if and when she decides to behave at home in the same way as she does at school, she'll be able to remove the diaper at home as well. There has been no change so far. I want to point out that my husband

has not been cooperative throughout this ordeal. He claims that the teacher and I rushed this process, despite the fact that the whole thing was initiated by my daughter, without any encouragement from me or the teacher. In any case, most of the day the child is with me. What can I do? Should I insist that my husband take part in the process?"

Answer Seventeen

Firstly, you must avoid creating any conflicts with the child, which can produce

a tense atmosphere surrounding the toilet-training process. Remember that the whole process is the child's own. It is an integral part of her development and she cannot be expected to accelerate or speed up the process simply because she showed signs of interest or went in the toilet at some point. Secondly, all efforts must involve not only you and the teacher but also the entire family. Thirdly, remember to praise and encourage the child every time she has a good toilet-training behavior. This must be done gently, so as not to send a message of expectation and demands. Finally, you

may want to meet with the teacher in order to identify the causes of her behavior and understand the reasons for the differences between the child's behavior at home and at daycare. Inviting the teacher to your home to interact with and encourage the child is certainly an option.

Further Reading for Parents and Children

Books for Children

Atkinson, Mary, ed. *My Potty Book for Boys*. New York: Dorling Kindersley, 2001. Explains toilet training for boys in simple words and pictures.

Atkinson, Mary, ed. *My Potty Book for Girls*. New York: Dorling Kindersley, 2001. Explains toilet training for girls in simple words and pictures.

Barrett, John E, and Jim Henson. *Too Big for Diapers: Featuring Jim Henson's Sesame Street Muppets*. New York: Random House, 2000. Baby Ernie receives a potty as a gift and learns how to use it.

Berenstain, Jan, and Stan Berenstain. *My Potty and I: A Friend in Need*. New York: Random House, 1999. A young bear tries his best to get to his potty chair on time, but he looks forward to the day when he will graduate to the big potty.

Cole, Joanna. *My Big Boy Potty*. New York: Harper Collins, 2000. With the help of his parents, a young boy learns to use his potty.

Cole, Joanna. *My Big Girl Potty*. New York: Harper Collins, 2000. Ashley learns to pee and poop in her potty and makes the transition from diapers to big-girl pants.

Ford, Bernette G, and Sam Williams. *No More Diapers for Ducky!*. London: Boxer Books, 2006. When Piggy can't

come out to play because he's busy sitting on the potty, Ducky realizes it's time to grow up, too.

Frankl, Alona. *Once Upon a Potty.* Woodbury: Barron's, 1984. This comes in two editions, one for boys and one for girls. It explains how and why a little boy (or girl) learns to use the potty.

Ingle, Annie, and Lisa McCue. *Lift the Lid, Use the Potty!.* New York: Random House, 2001. Little Bunny learns to use her brand new purple potty.

Lewison, Wendy Cheyette, and Richard E Brown. *The Princess and the Potty*. New York: Simon & Schuster Books for Young Readers, 1994. When everything fails to persuade the princess to use her potty, the king and queen consult the royal advisor who gives them valuable advice.

Miller, Virginia. *On Your Potty!*. Cambridge: Candlewick Press, 1998. Young bear Bartholomew finds that using his potty correctly is sometimes just a matter of the correct timing.

Mylo, Freeman. *Potty!* Berkeley: Tricycle Press, 2002.In the jungle sits a potty with the words "only the best bottom will fit on this potty," which prompts different animals to give it a try until a stranger shows them who fits it best.

Rogers, Paul, and Emma Rogers. *Ruby's potty*. New York: Dutton's Children's Books/Penguin Putnam Books for Young Readers, 2001. Ruby loves her brand new potty, but the trouble is that she doesn't know what it's for.

Ross, Anna, and Norman Gorbaty. *I Have to Go: Featuring Jim Henson's Sesame Street Muppets*. New York: Random House/Children's Television Workshop, 1990. Little Grover goes to the bathroom all by himself.

Van Genechten, Guido. *Potty Time*. New York: Simon & Schuster Books for Young Readers, 2001. Joe and his friends Nellie Elephant, Percy Pig, and Friendly Frog learn that, although bottoms come in all shapes and sizes, everyone must use the potty.

151

Willems, Mo. *Time to Pee!*. New York: Hyperion Books for Children, 2003. Sign-carrying mice give encouraging instructions for using the toilet. Each copy comes with a chart on the flip side of the book jacket and reward stickers for home use.

Books for Parents

Azrin, Nathan H, and Richard M Foxx. *Toilet Training in Less Than a Day*. New York: Simon and Schuster, 1974. From two noted learning specialists, this method teaches toilet training quickly.

Cole, Joanna. *Parents Book of Toilet Teaching*. New York: Ballantine Books, 1983. A comprehensive guide based on understanding your child's needs.

Mack, Alison, and George C Phillips. *Toilet Learning: The Picture Book Technique for Children and Parents*. Boston: Little, Brown, 1978. This includes separate discussions for parents and children about why and how to use a toilet.

Mackonochie, Alison. *Pee, Poop, and Potty Training*. Toronto: Firefly Books, 2003. This low-stress guide to toilet training

explains the basic plumbing of a baby's waste-disposal system, how to avoid diaper rashes, and how to prepare for potty training.

Mommy! I Have to Go Potty!: A Parent's Guide to Toilet Training. Seattle: Parenting Press, 2009. One of Parenting Press' most popular books, this reassuring guide to toddler and preschooler development has been updated and expanded by Helen F. Neville, a longtime pediatric advice nurse and parent educator.

Murkoff, Heidi Eisenberg, and Laura Rader. *What to Expect When You Use the Potty.* New York: Harper Festival, 2000. This book provides straightforward answers to you and your child's questions about the process of toilet training.

Rogers, Fred, and Jim Judkis. *Going to the Potty.* New York: Putnam, 1986. Rogers handles this sensitive subject with the same quiet candor and respect for young audiences that are the hallmark of his Mister Rogers' Neighborhood TV show. This book contains large color photos

of children using the toilet, and the tone is not overly cutesy or condescending. Children may be disappointed that Mr. Rogers himself appears only on the book's jacket, but parents will find this a valuable resource.

INDEX